Copyright © 1999 by Myles Munroe
Singles 101
ISBN 1-56229-130-0

Pneuma Life Publishing
P. O. Box 885
Lanham, Maryland 20703-0885
(301) 577-4052
http://www.pneumalife.com

Printed in the United States of America

Singles 101

Keys to Wholeness and Fulfillment

MYLES MUNROE

Pneuma Life Publishing

INTRODUCTION

Countless singles have fallen prey to the notion that because they are unmarried, they are therefore incomplete. Rather than celebrating that which makes them unique, many settle into the doldrums of loneliness and unfulfillment, all the while searching for that special someone to be their key to happiness.

In Singles 101, Dr. Myles Munroe recaptures God's plan for having a single, whole, and unique state of mind. He challenges singles to redeem their time wisely to become all that God has predestined, ordained, and called them to be—right now! Retrain and renew your mind with these precious insights as you pursue your purpose of living a full and satisfying life.

No human being can meet your ego, soul, or spiritual needs; you might as well settle all of that with God. You are only fit or ready for marriage when you are totally fulfilled in God.

Many have confused "singleness" with "being alone." Should there ever be a time when you cease to be a single being who is unique and whole? NO!

---

*If a "state of singleness" means
"to be unique and whole", then to be
totally single should be every
Christian's number one goal.*

No one should marry until he/she is totally single. Until you are a separate, single, unique and whole person, you are NOT ready to marry!

Instead of running from being single, you should be running toward singleness.

In Genesis 2:18, God said it's not good for man to be alone. He didn't say single. There is a profound difference between the two.

To not be alone, all you need is
some other humans to be your
companions and close friends.

Marriage was not instituted to solve

the problem of being alone—

human beings were created as an

answer to that problem.

*Many would be wise to consider
Adam in reference to singleness.
He was so totally unique and whole that
he did not miss anybody or even know
that he was alone.*

99% of marital problems arise because a husband or wife (or both) has not seen themselves as unique, worthy individuals—i.e., they had a bad self-image, were not whole or separate, but always depended on some other person to make them happy. They never maximized their singleness.

Marriage will not solve "aloneness."
There are many people who are in
non-working marriages where they pray to get
free, sleep in separate beds, or operate in
tension in their home. Marriages like that
create more aloneness than you—
as a single—could ever fathom.

God will not choose your mate for you.

If He did, that would violate your will

and power of choice.

If God chose your mate for you,

He would be taking responsibility

for your relationship; then if it failed,

the blame could be transferred to God.

God only presents, you choose.

Many are misguided by the misconception that God has created only one specific person on this planet for them to marry. That means the odds are one to five billion for you to find that "right one."

If God will and has chosen one individual out of five billion on this planet just for you, and did it without your knowledge and permission (and without the other person's), then why would He not choose salvation for you? That is a much more vital area of your life.

Whether or not you use the Word, wisdom, or the characteristics of God's nature to make your choice for a lifetime mate, you must take full responsibility for your choice and all the consequences that come with your decision.

Providing marriage prospects is God's responsibility, but choosing a mate is yours. Rely on the assistance of the Holy Spirit, but do not attempt to transfer the responsibility of choice to Him.

How much have you refined your separateness, uniqueness, and wholeness from others? Remember that a relationship is only as good as whatever the individuals involved bring to it.

If you are able to grasp the revelation of the difference between being "single" and being "alone," then you will never despise the state of being unmarried, and you will not marry based on wrong reasons.

Until you get to the state of being totally whole, totally unique, totally separate, with the knowledge that you don't need anyone to complete you, then you are not ready to marry.

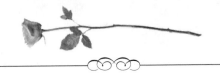

If you do not know who you are yet,

then why do you think you will find

yourself with someone else?

When you reach out frantically to others
for the wrong motives, you will exploit
and use them sexually, financially, or
emotionally to meet your own needs
without ever caring about theirs.

Many have set marriage and "living happily ever after" as their goal in life. The goal of the Christian is to become the separate, unique, and whole person the Lord wants you to become, and the vessel that will hold the Treasure, which is Jesus.

How you use time determines your life.

You are what you do with time.

No one can ever give you enough time or attention to make up for the emptiness where you are supposed to be full. If you are empty of a real self, then the other person will be unhappy because you have nothing to give back.

When you become consumed with being
who you are and focused on fulfilling your
purpose, then you will be ready to give up your
aloneness in favor of togetherness with someone
else who is separate, whole, and unique.

Your marriage will only be

as successful as your singleness, because

you can only bring to a marriage what you

are as a person alone.

Singleness is a myth. To be single means to be all one (alone), separate, unique and whole.

Before you love others,

you must love yourself first.

Find out who you are in Christ and as a person, then come to terms with that person. Knowing who you are is the first step toward wholeness, and accepting that person is the second step.

If you need to get married to be fulfilled or loved, you are not ready for marriage. The very thing that makes you need to get married will become the problem in your marriage.

In Matthew 22:39,

Jesus told the people to love their

neighbors as themselves. You cannot love

your neighbor if you have

no love for yourself.

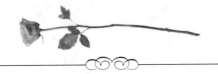

The next time someone says

to you, "I love you," try answering by

asking "But do you love you?"

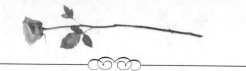

If you do not love yourself, you will look to someone else to make up up for that lack of love. You'll expect from that person more than they can possibly give in order to make up for what you lack within yourself.

*It is enough complication to develop
singleness while you are unmarried.
Why add complications to complication
by marrying an "un-single" person, and
then have two people in the same house
still trying to develop singleness?*

Do not let people rush you into getting married. Some people are not married yet because they were smart enough to not rush into like others.

Being single is the highest calling in the realm of relationships, because a successful marriage is only the product of two people being successfully single.

"I need a man." "I need a woman."

No, you need God and

you need your own holiness.

Today, God is saying, "Please get
your act together as an unmarried person.
Get your standards and values settled.
Build yourself on the Rock, Christ Jesus,
and set your feet on the bedrock of the
Word so that the pressures of
this world will not move you."

If you are yet unmarried, and you know that you do not want to live in that state for the rest of your life, then now is the time to become truly single so that your marriage will be successful in God.

You should build

"you"

before you ever think about

building a marriage.

Anyone who does not know
who he or she is becomes
fair game for someone else to
mold into another image.

"A merry heart doeth good like a medicine: but a broken spirit drieth the bones." (Prov. 17:22) Bones are the factories for blood, and life is in the blood. Anyone that touches your heart also touches your blood and therefore is touching your very life and existence.

You should not need someone else to make you whole, and you definitely should not enter into a marriage where the other person needs you to make him or her whole. Nobody has time to be dealing with an empty or half-empty spouse.

Solomon said,

"He who would have friends must
be friendly." (Proverbs 18:24)
That means that if you are lonely, then
it is because you are not friendly.

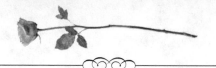

Are you afraid to be alone?
Some people always want other
people around because they do not like
themselves, or they are so empty that
they have to live through others.

*When alone, people who have
to constantly have the television or radio on
or involve themselves in reading or telephone
conversation are usually quite empty people
that seek to be filled with something or
somebody outside of themselves.*

God does not "choose" a mate for you.
However, if you ask Him, He will bring
along one that He knows is suitable for you
to choose. Your spouse must be of your
choosing——either to pick or accept——
or the marriage will not work.

Do not go "claiming"

a particular person to be your mate

without finding out God's opinion first.

Be wary of people "prophesying"
a mate for you—i.e., "So-and-so is to
marry So-and-so". Usually, that is wishful
thinking or someone else trying to impose
his thinking on you. In some cases, it is
even a trap set for you by Satan.

When you find yourself attracted to someone else, you had better find out why very quickly! It could be sensual; it could be that you feel that person fills an empty area in you; it could be you are feeling the pressure of the world to get married.

A person in a state of being single is a joy to the Lord. God has a special feeling for those that are satisfied and fulfilled with Him alone.

Unmarried Christians should be so consumed by God and His will, and so preoccupied and committed to finding out who they are in Him, that they are not distracted by the search for other people.

People who have not become truly single, who do not know who they are in Christ, or who do not have a firm identity of their own, will always reach for someone else to hold them up.

*If you choose an unmarried life
out of religious pressure, or false
spirituality, or being "disappointed
in love", then you are not giving God
a whole and truly single person.
You'll be cheating Him and yourself.*

*If you know the unmarried life
is not for you, then begin to ask
God to prepare you for marriage.
Ask Him to help you to become a
whole person, not a dependent leech.*

Do not slip into "losing yourself"
in someone else. You will become
a parasite and will either be sucking
life from them, or they will be
taking life from you.

"*I do not exist without you.*"
"*I can not get along without you.*"
"*If you go away, my world will crumble.*"
Those things are not romantic! That is
addictive dependency—instead of
an addictive substance, you are
addicted to a person.

Get prepared for marriage by yourself so
that you know for certain that no matter what
comes—storms, floods, the deepest valleys,
or the highest mountains—you will be able
to make it by yourself. Then you will be the
kind of person prepared to receive
the marriage vow.

The only people

God puts together are two people with

the Holy Spirit within them.

Everyone else, man marries.

You are not a "whole, single" being

who is prepared for marriage until

you are prepared never to get a divorce.

*Two born-again, spirit-filled believers
are qualified to marry each other
because they should be able to handle
problems through love and forgiveness and
through walking in the fruits of the Spirit.*

Do you have one eye on God and the other on the guys or girls? Then you are not totally whole yet. When both eyes are single-mindedly focused on the kingdom of God and His righteousness, then God will say: "Now, I see that it is not good for him or her to be alone. It is time for marriage."

True love is not a feeling;

it is a choice and a decision.

If you're thinking of getting married just for physical gratification, then know that your marriage shall be troubled from day one and will not last.

You are more effectively prepared for marriage when you do not "need" to be married. Your pursuit in life should not be marriage but "singlenes."

Shake yourself out of the
mode that causes you to casually or
traditionally consider marriage. Know
that marriage is the death and sacrifice of
exclusivity on the altar of love.

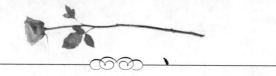

If you are considering marriage, are you willing to share your time, privacy, material goods, secrets, ambitions, dreams, goals, visions, and desires with another person?

Spend your time and energy
on the Lord and His work.
Preoccupy yourself with preparations
for the person God is preparing
to present to you.

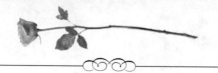

If you marry just because of passion,

your marriage will be passionately

destroyed eventually.

Whatever you feel is important and
necessary, yet it is still
causing you to sin, get rid of it.
It is harmful to you, not helpful.

As far as getting married is concerned,

do not join the army until you are prepared

to die and never defect.

If you are lonely, find someone else who is alone (not lonely or half-empty) and make friends. Begin to reach out to other successful people who are unmarried like you.

Do not love somebody just because they look nice—looks are subject to change. Love someone because of his or her attitude, character, and inner spirit being.

No matter how much you
love someone, find out if they serve God
and how they serve Him. Make sure
that you carry the same firewood to
burn on the same altar before
the same sacrifice.

Marriage is more than a legal contract to physically sleep together and share family financial obligations. Marriage is the joining and uniting of two souls wherein lies the center of submission, conviction, values, and moral and spiritual perceptions. If the souls are not compatible, the relationship is on the course of tragic disaster.

You may think now that
"love conquers all,"
but that is just until the
honeymoon is over!

Dating those who have different religions can cause problems. If what you believe is contrary to what the other person believes, you are headed for trouble.

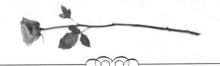

NEVER date a married person!!!
Do not set yourself up for emotional
turmoil by thinking you're only being
their confidant or "single" friend.

*If you see someone consistently,
then be careful because you are forming
"soul ties" or emotional bondings. You are
becoming dependent on one another
emotionally, even if not physically.*

Begin to take stock of your assets and

the advantages of the single life.

Are things really as bad as they seem?

If you readily detect that someone is not a prospective marriage partner, then why waste your time and energy dating, communicating and sharing your hopes, dreams, and inner thoughts with each other?

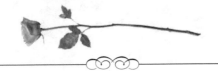

The minute you commit yourself
to someone else, then anything that
happens to break up that relationship
is an emotional divorce.

If you want to be successful, do not

keep company with failures.

Remember, iron sharpens iron.

Until you become whole, you will always be dependent on other people's opinions for your own self-worth.

Women, when you go out on dates, do not just sit there talking about mushy stuff. Ask your date what is his vision of you and what does he see in you, because whatever he sees is what he will cultivate.

You have to guard your heart

because out of is flows the issues of life.

Emotional bonding—whether positive

or negative—results in a loss

when it is broken.

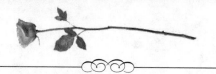

Instant relationships are no

guarantee of instant relief from

loneliness, pain, hurt feelings, or

damaged emotions.

Its okay to try to help friends

whose experiences you can identify

with, but not until you are at least on

the way to healing.

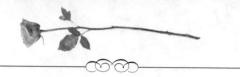

You are the result of your own use of time.

Whatever you did with your time in the

past has made you what you are today,

even your memories and regrets.

You can spend so much time

looking for who you want

that you have no time

to be who you are.

When a relationship fails, do not just move quickly to another one. There needs to be time to back off and see what your contribution was to the failed relationship.

If you have not changed for the better in some way from your relationship experiences, then what is to prevent your next relationship from going the same way, or worse?

*Hanging on to and being "friends"
with people you know are not God's best for
you or may be downright wrong for you is
a sure sign that you are weaving a security
blanket to cushion and comfort you from
emotional trauma. Your security and comfort
needs to be in Christ and the Word.*

Take custody of yourself.
Though you may have been hurt,
it's time for you to take responsibility
for restoring your life according to
God's principles and submit to
His healing process.

Take your roots out of other people

and develop the freedom to share

your fruit with them.

There is an old saying,

"*Marry in haste; repent at leisure.*"

That means you probably will be a

quite long time regretting your haste.

Just because you are not married yet, do not panic. Panic causes you to sell yourself short and always begins with a fear of some kind.

Developing soul ties is almost

like throwing cobwebs at one another

until you become totally enwebbed

in the other person.

There is no way you can ever

have peace in your heart if you live

your life just to find a mate.

You cannot live a healthy life and live in the past. Don't let failures of the past interfere with your future.

It is more important to be

"single" than to be married.

In fact, it is safer to be unmarried

than married, if you are not yet single.

Be truly single so that you can hear
the Lord about His will for you.
Marriage should never be for any
other motive, by either party,
than for God's will.

Men, before you go chasing a woman,

make sure she is someone you can chase

until death do you part.

Common presumptions about being "single" or "unmarried":

If you are single, then you are unmarried.

If you are unmarried, then you are single.

If you are unmarried, then you are incomplete.

If you are incomplete (unmarried), then you are unhappy.

If you are unhappy (unmarried), then you are depressed.

Consequently, the ridiculous presumption is that you are not happy until you are married.

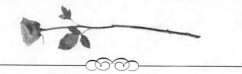

Marriage is not the key to happiness.

If marriage were the key to happiness, then

Jesus was depressed, Paul was frustrated,

and Ezekiel was a madman!

Singleness is an honor.

It is something that God gave you

first before anything else.

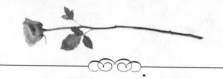

Singleness is not a temporary status.

It is a quality of life.

When you are unequivocally
single, you are whole and unique
in yourself and you know that you
are irreplaceable.

Redeem the time;

do not squander it away

doing foolish things.

Men work, cultivate, and protect.

Any man not fulfilling those

functions is malfunctioning.

Don't sit around sulking because you are unmarried. Make the most of every opportunity and maximize the moments you have in your life..

Time changes everything, but
you change everything by what you do
with the time you have. It will either
change things for the better or the worse
based on how you handle it.

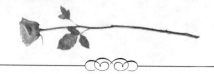

You can cause others to overcome by the word of your testimony. You can always tell where you are by whether or not you can talk freely about your experiences without pain, negative emotions, or entangling your mind again in sin.

Many are so busy looking for someone to be all things to them that they do not have time to be who they are. If you are too preoccupied looking for someone to be all things to you, then you will have no one and nothing to give them.

People are unmarried for different reasons. It does not mean that they are automatically sissies or that something is wrong with them. Understand now that it's okay to be unmarried.

Jesus said the greatest commandment is to love God with your whole heart, and the second greatest commandment is to love your neighbor to the same degree that you love yourself. Therefore, the key is loving you, not other people.

If you are not married and you are happy, stay happy. Only get married when you meet a person who can add to your happiness.

If you are not yet successful

at being single—if you cannot

control your emotions, your passions, your

feelings, your attitudes or your behavior—

then you are not prepared for marriage.

While you are unmarried, view marriage realistically. It is wonderful and has its rewards, but it is also full of challenges. It is wrong for you, as an unmarried individual, to view marriage as being the key to your happiness.

Marriage is not the prerequisite for your personal fulfillment.

It is critical that you not be in a hurry to get married. Relax, enjoy your life, and move in God.

Spend your time making plans for your

future, not hours reliving your past.

Many wonderful people have been
misguided by the misconception that
"unmarried" is equal to "singleness".
That is not true.

There are too many precious,
unmarried people that live a life full
of depression, frustration, and jealousy
because they have produced
self-imposed misery due to society's
pressures on them to be married.

Do not be so desperate

to get married that you grab

anything that comes along.

When you allow the pressure to get married to define you, you will execute irrational and poor judgement, and create a sense of desperation and fear because of your anxiousness to find a mate.

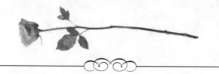

Do you conform to the world's standards?
Do you always have to busy yourself or
date on Friday or Saturday nights just to
prove that you are marketable?

There are people so bent on finding
someone that they do not spend any
time developing the person they want
to give to the person that they find.

Satan knows just how to get you and will maximize your misconceptions about marriage and singleness.

If you are so unhappy because all of your friends are married and you are still unmarried, then perhaps you should choose a married friend that will be real honest with you about whether or not they are truly "happily" married.

Marriage is not necessary for

the anointing or ministry.

Never develop a distrust and hatred of God simply because you blame Him for your own self-imposed misery due to the fact that you think you should be married by now.

The cry in most people's hearts who are unmarried is, "Jesus, You forgot me!" Let me tell you something, "He didn't forget you. He's protecting you!"

Complete people are the most interesting people in the world. Those who have a vision, goals, purposes, and plans for their lives are the most attractive. A whole person knows who he is, why he is at a certain place, where he is going, and how he is going to get there.

When you are truly "single", you know
that you are different from everybody else,
and you have a wholeness that can be
shared with other people.

Let's get this straight: To be single means you are a separate, unique, and whole person. To be unmarried means that you are not married—you aren't committed in matrimonial covenant with another person. Don't add negative connotations to either state of being single or unmarried.

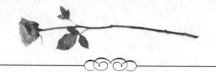

Make yourself so single that someone

has to single you out to touch you.

If you haven't mastered your singleness, then the fact that you are not a whole and unique person with no good self-concept will always show up in your relationships.

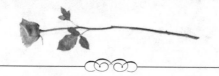

Singleness creates a sense of value within yourself. It causes you and others to regard you highly.

Do not allow the devil to turn you into a self-hater with a jealous spirit just because you are unmarried.

Marriage myths:

Marriage is the key to happiness.

Marriage is the key to completeness.

Marriage is the key to fulfillment.

Marriage is the solution to loneliness.

Marriage is necessary for spiritual maturity or leadership.

Marriage creates love.

Marriage is not necessary to

go to heaven just in case you do not

want Jesus to come back until

you get married.

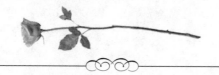

The Bible teaches us that you should be married to have a child; but you do not need to be married to be a mentor.

When you truly value yourself, you will never sell yourself cheaply.

Enjoy your unmarried state, and

while you are unmarried,

develop your singleness.

There is no way that a person is totally "single" before you marry them, but, you ought to at least make sure that a lot of the work is done before you have got to work on them. You do not want to start from scratch!

Make sure that the person you marry is whole. Life is too short for you to spend your life on baby-sitting somebody. You want to be a husband or a wife to someone, not their Mommy or Daddy.

The more single you become, the

more you will protect yourself

from people using you.

If you are not married, it is important for you to concentrate on being single more than on being married because marriage exposes your lack of "singleness."

*If you are not careful, you will waste
years worrying and being preoccupied
with pursuing prospective mates at
the expense of your own personal
development and refinement.*

You do not want to marry someone that you have to constantly pull up. You want someone that is able to walk with you in agreement. The Bible says, "Can two walk together except they be agreed?" Amos 3:3

When you work hard on yourself,

educating yourself, and fixing yourself

up, you cause others that want to be with

you to "come up a little higher!"

OTHER BOOKS TITLES IN 101 SERIES

WIFE 101
HUSBAND 101
MARRIAGE 101
WEIGHT LOSS 101
SEX 101
CHRISTIAN LIFE 101